Barber, Terry, 195
Muhammad Ali /
c2007
3330525962
gi   0 13 17

W9-CSR-508

Muhammad Ali

Terry Barber

SPORTS
SERIES

Text copyright © 2007 Terry Barber

Photographs copyright © in the names of individual photographers, artists, and organizations as noted specifically on page 51.

All rights reserved. No part of this book may be reproduced or transmitted in any form or by an means, including photocopy, recording, or any information storage and retrieval system, without the prior written permission of the publisher.

Muhammad Ali is published by
Grass Roots Press, a division of Literacy Services of Canada Ltd.

www.grassrootsbooks.net

ACKNOWLEDGMENTS

We acknowledge the financial support of the Government of Canada through the Canada Book Fund (CBF) for our publishing activities.

Produced with the assistance of
the Government of Alberta, Alberta
Multimedia Development Fund.

Alberta
Government

Editor: Dr. Pat Campbell
Image research: Dr. Pat Campbell
Book design: Lara Minja, Lime Design Inc.

Library and Archives Canada Cataloguing in Publication

Barber, Terry, date
    Muhammad Ali / Terry Barber.

ISBN 978-1-894593-58-8

    1. Ali, Muhammad, 1942– . 2. Boxers (Sports)—United States—Biography. 3. Readers for new literates. I. Title.

PE1126.N43B3634 2007   428.6'2   C2007-902538-2

Contents

A thief steals the boy's bike.

A Boy Learns to Box

The boy is 12 years old. The boy is mad. The boy is in tears. His new bike is gone. A thief stole his bike. The boy looks for a cop. He finds a cop in a boxing gym.

A boxing gym.

A Boy Learns to Box

The boy tells the cop about his bike. The boy says he wants to beat up the thief. The cop says, "You better learn how to fight." The cop is also a boxing coach. He teaches the boy to box.

Cassius Clay at the age of 12.

A Boy Learns to Box

The boy is Cassius Clay. Boxing is a hard sport to learn. Clay learns fast. In a few weeks, Clay wins his first fight. Over the next six years, Clay wins many fights. He wins six Golden Gloves titles in Kentucky.

Clay is born in Louisville, Kentucky on January 17, 1942.

Clay writes a poem in 1963.
(Clay's mother is on the left.)

A Boy Learns to Box

Clay likes to write poetry. He writes his first poem when he is 12. He writes poems about life. He writes poems about other boxers. Clay reads his poems before he fights. Fans love Clay's poems.

This is Clay's first poem: "This guy is done. I'll stop him in one."

Clay trains with another boxer.

Dreams and Goals

Clay has a dream. He wants to be the world's best boxer. Clay works hard to reach his dream. He trains six days a week. He does not smoke. He does not drink.

Clay wears his gold medal at the Olympics.

Dreams and Goals

Clay has a goal. He wants to go to the Olympics. He wants to win a gold medal. Clay trains hard. He boxes at the 1960 Olympics. Clay wins a gold medal.

Clay returns home. He walks into an eating place for whites only. Clay is not served. He gets mad. Clay throws his gold medal in the river.

Clay "floats like a butterfly and stings like a bee."

Clay Turns Pro

Clay turns pro. His boxing gets better and better. He is quick on his feet. He throws fast punches from all angles. Clay rarely gets hit. Clay "floats like a butterfly and stings like a bee."

Clay trains to become world champion.

Clay Turns Pro

It is 1964. Cassius Clay is 22 years old. Clay has been a pro boxer for four years. He has not lost a fight. Clay has a new goal. He wants to be the world champion.

Clay wants to put a collar and rope on the "bear."

World Champion

Clay stands over Liston.

Sonny Liston is the world champion. Clay must win the title from Liston. Clay calls Liston a "big, ugly bear." Most people think Clay will lose the fight. These people are wrong. Clay wins the world championship on February 25, 1964.

Clay says, "I am the greatest."

Ali waves to his fans.

World Champion

Clay shakes up the world with his win. A few days later, Clay shakes up the world even more. Clay changes his name to Muhammad Ali. Clay is a slave name. Ali is a name that sets him free.

Ali thinks black slaves got the name "Clay" from white men.

Black people are treated like second-class citizens.

Ali Fights Racism

In the 1960s, many black people are treated like second-class citizens. Muhammad Ali will not put up with this. Ali says: "I am America. I am the past you won't recognize. But get used to me: black, confident, **cocky**."

Ali speaks to people about equal rights.

Ali Fights Racism

Ali is not like most black boxing
champions. Most black champions
fight in the ring. Ali fights outside the
ring too. He uses his fame to fight
racism. He talks about how hard it is
to be a black American.

These people protest the war.

The Vietnam War

The U.S. is at war with Vietnam.
Americans must serve in the armed
forces. They are sent to Vietnam to
fight. Many American soldiers die.
Many people in the U.S. **protest** the
war.

The
Vietnam War
goes from 1961
to 1975.

Ali does not want to serve in the Army.

The Vietnam War

Ali does not want to serve in the
Army. Ali does not want to kill people.
In the U.S., black people cannot buy
a cup of coffee in some places. Why
should a black man risk his life for the
U.S.?

Ali says:
"I ain't got no
quarrel with those
Viet Cong."

Ali is sad about his losses.

The Vietnam War

Ali pays a big price for not going to war. In 1967, Ali loses his licence to box. He loses his world boxing title. Ali gets a $10,000 fine.

Ali gives a speech.

The Vietnam War

Ali does not box for 3 ½ years.
But his fame grows. Ali gives speeches.
He talks about life. He talks about
civil rights. He talks about black pride.
Ali becomes a hero of the people.

Ali takes a punch from Joe Frazier at the 1971 title fight.

Ali Returns
to the Ring

In 1970, Ali is allowed to box again. Ali is not the same boxer. He used to take pride in not getting hit. Now he takes pride in being able to take a punch. He used to float like a butterfly. Now he floats more like a bee.

Ali becomes champion for the third time.

Ali Returns to the Ring

Ali is still a good boxer. He wins the
world boxing title two more times.
Ali's skills begin to **fade**. But his
courage never leaves him. Now,
Ali's courage helps him to win fights.

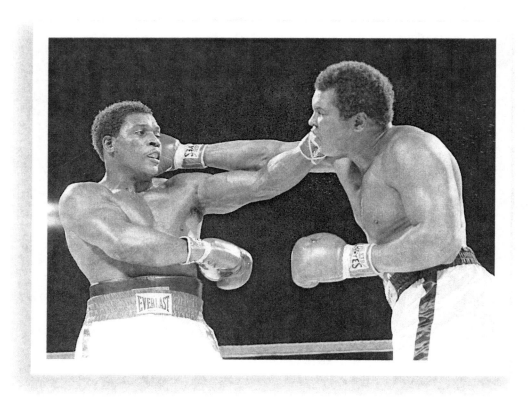

Ali fights Berbick in 1981.

Ali Returns to the Ring

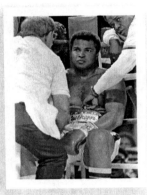

Ali takes a rest
at his last fight.

Ali's last fight is in 1981. He loses to Trevor Berbick.

Berbick is a little bit better than Ali at his worst. Ali's fans are happy to see him retire. Ali's fans do not want him to get hurt.

Ali's pro record is 56 wins – 5 losses.

Ali lights the flame at the 1996 Olympics.

More Than a Boxer

Ali goes to the Olympics in 1996. People around the world watch him light the Olympic flame. He gets a special gold medal. It replaces the medal he threw in the river.

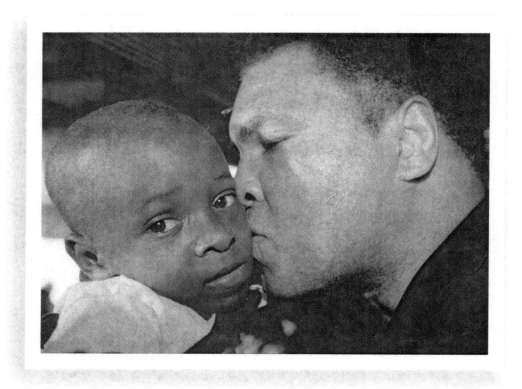

Ali kisses an orphan in Africa.

More Than a Boxer

Ali never found the thief who took his bike. He found magic in a boxing gym. The name Ali is known around the world. Ali may be the best boxer ever.

We will also remember Ali for his work outside the ring.

Glossary

cocky: very sure of oneself.

fade: to slowly disappear.

protest: to complain about something.

quarrel: an angry argument.

racism: a belief that one race is superior to others.

Viet Cong: a member of the Communist guerilla movement in Vietnam.

Talking About the Book

What did you learn about Muhammad Ali?

Why did Ali throw his gold medal in the river?

Ali says: "I am America. I am the past you won't recognize. But get used to me: black, confident, cocky." What do you think this means?

Why didn't Ali want to serve in the Vietnam war?

Why do you think Ali was a hero of the people?

Picture Credits

Front cover photos (center photo): © Library of Congress. Prints and Photographs Division, LC-USZ62-115435; **(small photo):** © AP. **Contents page (top right):** © AP/ George Brich; **(bottom left):** © Library of Congress. Prints and Photographs Division, LC-USZ62-121468; **(bottom right);** © CP. **Page 4:** Leon Dixon/NBHAA. **Page 6:** © AP/ Robert Kradin. **Page 8:** © AP. **Page 10:** © AP. **Page 12:** © AP. **Page 14:** © AP. **Page 16:** © AP/ H.B. Littell. **Page 18:** © Harry Benson/Hulton Archive/ Getty Images. **Page 19:** © Library of Congress. Prints and Photographs Division, LC-USZ62-115784. **Page 20:** © AP/ Frank C. Curtin. **Page 21:** © Library of Congress. Prints and Photographs Division. LC-USZ62-120902. **Page 22:** © AP. **Page 24:** © AP. **Page 26:** © AP. **Page 28:** © Library of Congress. Prints and Photographs Division, LC-USZ62-121468. **Page 30:** © AP. **Page 32:** © AP. **Page 34:** © AP/ George Brich. **Page 36:** © CP/Everett Collection. **Page 38:** © AP. **Page 40:** © CP. **Page 41:** © AP. **Page 42:** © CP. **Page 44:** © AP/ David Guttenfelder.

CPSIA information can be obtained at www.ICGtesting.com
Printed in the USA
LVOW09s2340031016

507279LV00005B/49/P

9 781894 593588